The path to achieving a goal is always accompanied by dangers, difficulties, and discomforts. Energy and eagerness present a formidable foe against obstacles. To learn about how people across the world are using enthusiasm to achieve extraordinary things or to share your story of grit and gumption, please email me at fox@foxbeyer.com.

Adapt and Maintain Enthusiasm in Adversity

Using the 5-Step F.A.C.T.S. Process to Find
Your Strength and Enthusiasm to Succeed

Fox Beyer

THiNKaha®

An Actionable Success Journal

E-mail: info@thinkaha.com
20660 Stevens Creek Blvd., Suite 210
Cupertino, CA 95014

Please go to
https://aha.pub/FACTS
to read this AHAbook and to share the
individual AHAmessages that resonate with you.

Published by THiNKaha®
20660 Stevens Creek Blvd., Suite 210,
Cupertino, CA 95014
https://thinkaha.com
E-mail: **info@thinkaha.com**

Second Printing: July 2020
First Printing: June 2020
Hardcover ISBN: 978-1-61699-372-6   1-61699-372-3
Paperback ISBN: 978-1-61699-371-9   1-61699-371-5
eBook ISBN: 978-1-61699-370-2   1-61699-370-7
Place of Publication: Silicon Valley, California, USA
Paperback Library of Congress Number: 2020907218

Dedication

To my family, friends, coaches, mentors, colleagues, teachers, Whippany Park High School, the Somerset Patriots, and the University of South Carolina, your impact on me is infinite and no doubt evident on the upcoming pages. Thank you!

Acknowledgements

I wish to recognize a group of people who without their relentless guidance and genuine concern, this book would have never been possible. Mitchell Levy, Jenilee Maniti, Kharen Basa, and to the whole "AHAthat/THiNKaha Team"— I appreciate you.

How to Read a THiNKaha® Book

A Note from the Publisher

The AHAthat/THiNKaha series is the CliffsNotes of the 21st century. These books are contextual in nature. Although the actual words won't change, their meaning will every time you read one as your context will change. Be ready, you will experience your own AHA moments as you read the AHA messages™ in this book. They are designed to be stand-alone actionable messages that will help you think about a project you're working on, an event, a sales deal, a personal issue, etc., differently. As you read this book, please think about the following:

1. It should only take 15–20 minutes to read this book the first time out. When you're reading, write in the underlined area one to three action items that resonate with you.
2. Mark your calendar to re-read this book again in 30 days.
3. Repeat step #1 and mark one to three more AHA messages that resonate. They will most likely be different than the first time. BTW: this is also a great time to reflect on the AHA messages that resonated with you during your last reading.

After reading a THiNKaha book, marking your AHA messages, re-reading it, and marking more AHA messages, you'll begin to see how these books contextually apply to you. AHAthat/THiNKaha books advocate for continuous, lifelong learning. They will help you transform your AHAs into actionable items with tangible results until you no longer have to say AHA to these moments—they'll become part of your daily practice as you continue to grow and learn.

Mitchell Levy, Global Credibility Expert
publisher@thinkaha.com

Contents

Foreword

In the fall of 1997, Fox and I were walking through the campus of the University of South Carolina. Both of us were students there, and we were talking about our dinner menu for the upcoming Thanksgiving break. We were side by side, mouths watering with the talk of turkey, stuffing, and all the fixings. As I continued the conversation, I was surprised to notice that Fox was no longer beside me. I turned around to see him doing push-ups on the sidewalk, counting each repetition. I began to laugh uncontrollably.

Fox had tripped over a crack in the sidewalk.

But he didn't cry, complain, or look around and become embarrassed. Instead, he took ownership of the situation. He learned from an early age that he had to strengthen his upper body in order to catch himself and avoid injury during these frequent circumstances. I didn't laugh at Fox because I was making fun of him. I laughed at what he learned to do after the inevitable: have fun with it, turn an obstacle into a positive, and heck, get some exercise. That's what he wants to help us learn too.

Time and again, Fox has shown the ability to outwit doctors and other medical professionals—he was certainly named appropriately. Through countless surgeries and complications, he has always managed to find a way to overcome these obstacles, to the constant amazement of all around him. Through this book, Fox presents ways for the reader to deal with adversity, maintain enthusiasm through any circumstance, and improve overall feelings of self-worth. No one has to experience the physical battles he continues to go through to benefit from this book. We all experience everyday struggles that could use uplifting.

There is not a person whom I feel is more authentic, more caring of others, more resilient, or more honest than Fox. He truly blazes a trail of fresh thinking that is relatable to everyone at any stage or emotion in life. I am truly proud and fortunate to be able to have a friend, or better yet, a brother, in Fox Beyer.

Brett Jodie
Manager, Somerset Patriots

Introduction

It was June 2002. To my utter delight, the University of South Carolina baseball program had returned to the College World Series after a seventeen-year hiatus. As a student coach on that team, I found myself standing in the dugout during team introductions before our first game against Georgia Tech, which was being nationally televised on ESPN. While anxiously waiting for my name to be called, I kept telling myself:

"Fox, bend your legs at the hips."
"Stand up straight, for goodness' sake."
"Run heel-toe."

Finally, the climactic moment arrived.

"Student coach, Fox Beyer," blared the Rosenblatt Stadium loudspeaker. I began to run toward the first-base foul line. After a few steps, I tripped, fell forward, and caught myself with my hands. It was not an ideal entrance, but my hands have always been there for me—both in June 2002 and in July 1997, when I threw out the ceremonial first pitch of a New York Yankees' game. Yes, that day, while entering the field, I again tripped, fell forward, and caught myself with my hands.

Again, that was not part of my plan. But, did I eventually join my Gamecock teammates on the first-base line? Yes. Did I eventually throw out that first pitch? Yes.

Today, I look at my hands and I'm thankful. I'm thankful for people like my parents and therapists, who knew that as a kid growing up with cerebral palsy, I was going to fall every day of my life. They also understood that 99 percent of my falls were forward. Knowing this, I trained constantly to put my hands out in front of my body as I fell, protecting myself from further harm. Today, as a teacher and coach, I reflect on many of my infamous tumbles, what they've taught me, and how I can use them to help you.

Life is full of **adversity**—and having the **enthusiasm** to overcome it.

The pages that follow contain 140 AHA messages, each one related to an obstacle-surmounting perspective whose key words unite to form the acronym, F.A.C.T.S. Be ready when shit hits the fan!

The tougher the challenge, the more special the person. #Grit #Enthusiasm

Fox Beyer
https://aha.pub/FACTS

Share the AHA messages from this book socially by going to
https://aha.pub/FACTS.

Section I

F-Realize That When You Fail, It Doesn't Make You a **Failure**

Is the road to success paved? NO! Do failures accompany the ride? YES! Is enthusiasm a key part of the journey? YOU BET! By understanding that obstacles will be full of struggle, we are more apt to focus on the process, learn from inevitable disappointments, and maintain an enthusiastic approach.

F — Understand that when you FAIL, it doesn't make you a failure.

A — Embrace your AUTHENTICITY. Let people see your quirks and insecurities.

C — Learn from others, rather than COMPARING yourself to them.

T — "TURN off the noise" to allow the "white space"

S — Find SOMEONE you trust, who listens/builds you up/breaks you down when needed.

1

The road to success is not paved. #Grit #Enthusiasm

_____

_____

_____

2

The tougher the challenge, the more special the person. #Grit #Enthusiasm

_____

_____

_____

3

The struggles you face are real, and you can tell them to
kiss your @$$. #Grit #Enthusiasm

_____

_____

_____

4

The victory highway is not smooth sailing. That road is a
constant uphill battle. #Grit #Enthusiasm

_____

_____

_____

5

Marry yourself to a trait called resilience.
#Grit #Enthusiasm

_____

_____

_____

6

Harping on failures robs you of the #Enthusiasm needed
to conquer obstacles. #Grit

_____

_____

_____

7

Perceive obstacles as opportunities to adapt and grow.
#Grit #Enthusiasm

_____

_____

_____

8

Be someone of integrity, and you'll always be at your
best. #Grit #Enthusiasm

_____

_____

_____

9

Have you done all you can do? Are you ready for what is to come? You'll have to adjust and adapt. #Grit #Enthusiasm

_____

_____

_____

10

Count your blessings. If you don't have them, adjust and adapt to work things out. #Grit #Enthusiasm

_____

_____

_____

11

When you are dealt a second-rate hand, it comes down to the character of the person. #Grit #Enthusiasm

_____

_____

_____

12

Mental makeup and humility are ultimate intangibles, akin to #Enthusiasm. #Grit

_____

_____

_____

13

#Enthusiasm is a key element in the journey THROUGH failure. #Grit

_____

_____

_____

14

All in doesn't mean all smooth.
—Martin Kelly via https://aha.pub/FoxBeyer
#Grit #Enthusiasm

_____

_____

_____

15

Write down YOUR definition of success. It will set a clear direction, make you less likely to dwell on inevitable failures, and give you more #Enthusiasm. #Grit

_____

_____

_____

16

Conquer weakness to become great. #Grit #Enthusiasm

_____

_____

_____

17

One of life's greatest teachers is experience.
#Grit #Enthusiasm

_____

_____

_____

18

Embrace your character. #Grit #Enthusiasm

_____

_____

_____

19

Tough beginnings are pit-stops in life. The victory highway
is full of struggle and strife. #Grit #Enthusiasm

_____

_____

_____

20

At the beginning of each day, give your struggles a
game-faced salutation. #Grit #Enthusiasm

_____

_____

_____

21

No one is a stranger to the tough and unforgiving.
#Grit #Enthusiasm

_____

_____

_____

22

Accomplishments are often accompanied by challenges.
#Grit #Enthusiasm

_____

_____

_____

23

Q.T.L.= Quality Time Lived. Adversity included.
#Grit #Enthusiasm

_____

_____

_____

24

Success is the culmination of learning from many failures.
#Grit #Enthusiasm

_____

_____

_____

25

Difficulties exist to be overcome. #Grit #Enthusiasm

_____

_____

_____

26

Failures have way of teaching us to become better leaders. #Grit #Enthusiasm

_____

_____

_____

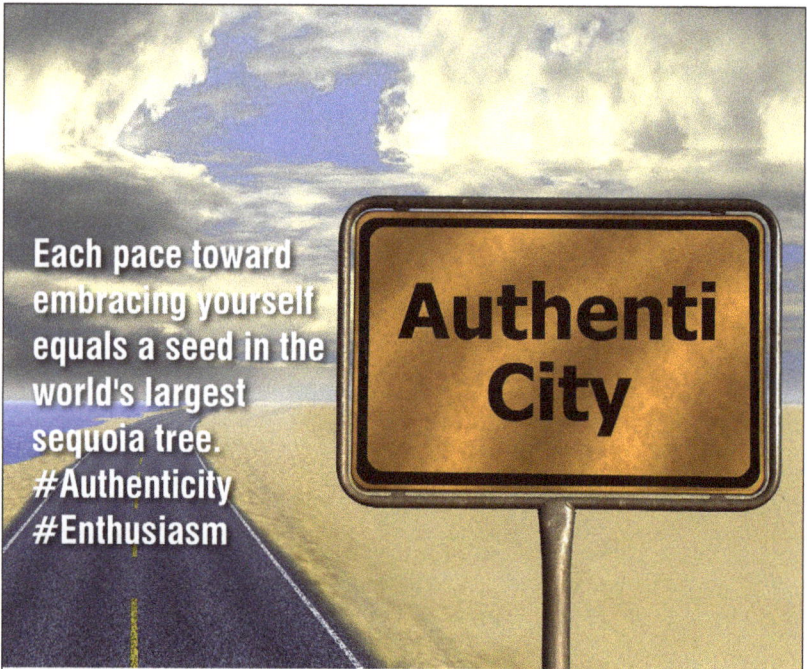

Each pace toward embracing yourself equals a seed in the world's largest sequoia tree. #Authenticity #Enthusiasm

Authenti City

Fox Beyer
https://aha.pub/FACTS

Share the AHA messages from this book socially by going to
https://aha.pub/FACTS.

Section II

A-Embrace Your **Authenticity**

Do we all have doubts and insecurities? YES! Does masking them in the face of adversity rob you of valuable enthusiasm? YES! By showing our vulnerabilities in adversity, we encourage others to do the same, thereby strengthening the team around us while maintaining enthusiasm.

F — Understand that when you FAIL, it doesn't make you a failure.

A — Embrace your AUTHENTICITY. Let people see your quirks and insecurities.

C — Learn from others, rather than COMPARING yourself to them.

T — "TURN off the noise" to allow the "white space"

S — Find SOMEONE you trust, who listens/builds you up/breaks you down when needed.

27

You can sometimes hide from the outside world, but the mirror always shows the truth. #Authenticity #Enthusiasm

_____

_____

_____

28

From the moment we were conceived, we were genetically designed to be different. Don't waste #Enthusiasm trying to be someone you are not. #Authenticity

_____

_____

_____

29

We all have insecurities. When we mask them, we waste energy and drain ourselves of #Enthusiasm. #Authenticity

_____

_____

_____

30

With so many similar variables, remember how you were made. Remember that your individuality is saved. #Authenticity #Enthusiasm

_____

_____

_____

31

Instead of masking fears in the name of practicality, perceive fear as opportunity. #Authenticity #Enthusiasm

_____

_____

_____

32

Masking fears drains you of the #Enthusiasm needed to conquer them. #Authenticity

_____

_____

_____

33

Each pace toward embracing yourself equals a seed in the world's largest sequoia tree. #Authenticity #Enthusiasm

_____

_____

_____

34

Admitting your insecurities instills a feeling of winning tranquility within the body and mind — and bolsters #Enthusiasm and #Authenticity

_____

_____

_____

35

We all have "screws loose."
If we didn't, we wouldn't be normal.
—Robert Andino via https://aha.pub/FoxBeyer
#Authenticity #Enthusiasm

_____

_____

_____

36

Show past your skin. Show what lies within.
#Authenticity #Enthusiasm

_____

_____

_____

37

You are the sum of all your parts. Embracing them further
fills your #Enthusiasm's cup. #Authenticity

_____

_____

_____

38

Inside and out, you are scientifically proven to be
unmatched. #Authenticity #Enthusiasm

_____

_____

_____

39

It's not your fame but your imprint that makes you different. Embrace it. #Authenticity #Enthusiasm

_____

_____

_____

40

You can inspire others by simply being yourself.
#Authenticity #Enthusiasm

_____

_____

_____

41

Diverse. Particular. You. #Authenticity #Enthusiasm

_____

_____

_____

42

Open your door. Let others in. #Authenticity #Enthusiasm

_____

_____

_____

43

Being selfish and loving yourself are two different things.
#Authenticity #Enthusiasm

_____

_____

_____

44

Own Your YOU. #Authenticity #Enthusiasm

_____

_____

_____

45

One way to cope with insecurity is admitting it or showing it plainly. #Authenticity #Enthusiasm

_____

_____

_____

46

Be polite. Laugh. Realize we all sin. Admit and learn.
#Authenticity #Enthusiasm

_____

_____

_____

47

By showing our emotional vulnerabilities in adversity, we
encourage others to do the same, thereby strengthening
the team around us. #Authenticity #Enthusiasm

_____

_____

_____

48

Transparency leads to human connectivity.
#Authenticity #Enthusiasm

_____

_____

_____

49

The true you represents encouragement for others.
Encouragement represents a great form of motivation.
#Authenticity #Enthusiasm

_____

_____

_____

50

The more secure admit their insecurities.
#Authenticity #Enthusiasm

51

Free others by showing your own vulnerability.
#Authenticity #Enthusiasm

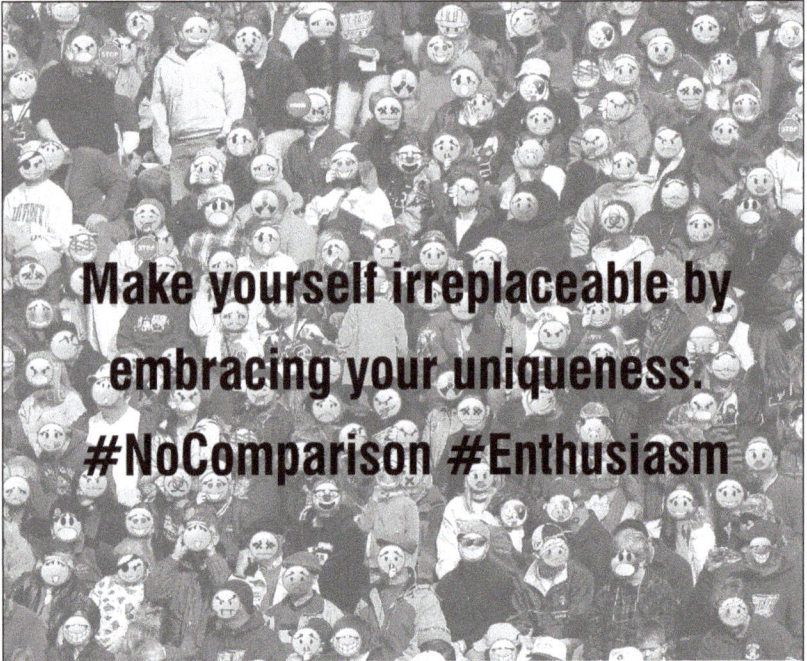

Make yourself irreplaceable by embracing your uniqueness. #NoComparison #Enthusiasm

Fox Beyer
https://aha.pub/FACTS

Share the AHA messages from this book socially by going to
https://aha.pub/FACTS.

Section III

C-Don't **Compare** Yourself with Others

Are comparisons often unrealistic and unfair? YES! Are they enthusiasm's blood-sucking leeches? YES! By eliminating comparisons, focusing on strengths, and developing OUR version of others' admirable traits, enthusiasm is utilized, not destroyed.

F — Understand that when you FAIL, it doesn't make you a failure.

A — Embrace your AUTHENTICITY. Let people see your quirks and insecurities.

C — Learn from others, rather than COMPARING yourself to them.

T — "TURN off the noise" to allow the "white space"

S — Find SOMEONE you trust, who listens/builds you up/breaks you down when needed.

52

Replace comparing yourself to others with taking pride in yourself. #NoComparison #Enthusiasm

_____

_____

_____

53

Use what you learn from others to make a better you.
#NoComparison #Enthusiasm

_____

_____

_____

54

Think of someone you admire. Write down one of their characteristics. Devise ways to personally develop this characteristic every day. #NoComparison #Enthusiasm

_____

_____

_____

55

Instead of comparing yourself to others, learn from them. Sometimes, they'll show you what not to do. #NoComparison #Enthusiasm

_____

_____

_____

56

Replace comparisons with positive self talk.
#NoComparison #Enthusiasm

_____

_____

_____

57

Constantly comparing yourself to others is to discount
what makes you unique. #NoComparison #Enthusiasm

_____

_____

_____

58

Make yourself irreplaceable by embracing your uniqueness. #NoComparison #Enthusiasm

_____

_____

_____

59

Invest time in learning from others instead of
spending your time comparing yourself to them.
#NoComparison #Enthusiasm

_____

_____

_____

60

Often, comparisons create unrealistic expectations.
#NoComparison #Enthusiasm

_____

_____

_____

61

Learn from others and adjust your approach.
#NoComparison #Enthusiasm

_____

_____

_____

62

Replace comparisons with subconscious positive images.
#NoComparison #Enthusiasm

_____

_____

_____

63

Instead of doing it like someone else,
do it for someone else. Servant leadership breeds
#Enthusiasm. #NoComparison

_____

_____

_____

64

If you are running a race and look around to see where
your competitors are, you are likely to slow down.
#NoComparison #Enthusiasm

_____

_____

_____

65

Instead of growing like others, allow others to help you grow. #NoComparison #Enthusiasm

_____

_____

_____

66

Stop comparing yourself to others. Never, however, stop learning from them. #NoComparison #Enthusiasm

_____

_____

_____

67

Comparison is the thief of you.
—Clint Hurdle via https://aha.pub/FoxBeyer
#NoComparison #Enthusiasm

_____

_____

_____

68

The more time you spend comparing yourself to others, the less time you spend getting to know yourself.
#NoComparison #Enthusiasm

_____

_____

_____

69

Don't compare. Embrace. Change. Adapt.
#NoComparison #Enthusiasm

_____

_____

_____

70

Comparisons are often judgments that lead to self-deprecation. #NoComparison #Enthusiasm

_____

_____

_____

71

Comparisons often lead to anxiety. Change is easier if you relax. If you can't relax, it's hard to adjust. #NoComparison #Enthusiasm

_____

_____

_____

72

Fray the line between the impossible and the possible by doing it your way. #NoComparison #Enthusiasm

_____

_____

_____

73

Comparisons are often unfair and unrealistic and drain you of #Enthusiasm. #NoComparison

_____

_____

_____

74

Replace comparisons with a desire to evolve.
#NoComparison #Enthusiasm

_____

_____

_____

75

Eliminating comparison is, in itself, a form of
encouragement. #NoComparison #Enthusiasm

_____

_____

_____

Sitting in #Silence for periods during the day is like filling up at a gas pump for the mind — and it doesn't cost a thing. #Enthusiasm

Fox Beyer

https://aha.pub/FACTS

Share the AHA messages from this book socially by going to
https://aha.pub/FACTS.

Section IV

T-**Turn Off the Noise** to Allow the White Space

Do we need to refuel enthusiasm's tank in times of struggle? YES! What's a way to do this and immediately return to a task with vigor? Practice silence. In silence, we can calmly devise ways to be more efficient and productive in spite of circumstances out of our control.

F — Understand that when you FAIL, it doesn't make you a failure.

A — Embrace your AUTHENTICITY. Let people see your quirks and insecurities.

C — Learn from others, rather than COMPARING yourself to them.

T — "TURN off the noise" to allow the "white space"

S — Find SOMEONE you trust, who listens/builds you up/breaks you down when needed.

76

Detach. You'll return to a task with a renewed vigor.
#Silence #Enthusiasm

_____

_____

_____

77

Sitting in #Silence for periods during the day is like filling
up at a gas pump for the mind — and it doesn't cost a
thing. #Enthusiasm

_____

_____

_____

78

Replace complaining with #Silence or meditation.
You'll become more attractive to others
and spread #Enthusiasm.

_____

_____

_____

79

When you are angry or irritable, stop. Think.
Is it because you didn't give yourself enough downtime?
#Silence #Enthusiasm

_____

_____

_____

80

You'll be less distracted by the inevitable noise in your life if you allot time to enjoy #Silence during the day. #Enthusiasm

_____

_____

_____

81

#Silence is rest. Rest gives us fuel to perform optimally. #Enthusiasm

_____

_____

_____

82

Make #Silence an integral part of your daily routine.
#Enthusiasm

_____

_____

_____

83

Let #Silence lead to efficiency,
and efficiency will lead to productivity. #Enthusiasm

_____

_____

_____

84

Regularly check in with the most valuable resource you have: your mind. It's where #Enthusiasm lives. #Silence

_____

_____

_____

85

Whining or #Silence? Which one benefits you and others as well? #Enthusiasm

_____

_____

_____

86

Complaining makes a bad situation worse. Allow white space and begin to devise ways to fix the situation.
—Bill Beyer via https://aha.pub/FoxBeyer
#Silence #Enthusiasm

_____

_____

_____

87

How will you know how effective #Silence and meditation are for you? Try them. Make the investment. It is sure to pay dividends. #Enthusiasm

_____

_____

_____

88

Gain control over yourself. Indulge in #Silence regularly.
#Enthusiasm

_____

_____

_____

89

Access your inner strength. #Silence #Enthusiasm

_____

_____

_____

90

Shed your baggage. Meditate. #Silence #Enthusiasm

_____

_____

_____

91

Two eyes. One mouth. Observe. #Silence #Enthusiasm

_____

_____

_____

92

A walk outside will give you a bevy of ideas to choose from and worthwhile ways to direct your #Enthusiasm. #Silence

_____

_____

_____

93

#Silence has a way of undisguising your ideas. #Enthusiasm

_____

_____

_____

94

Fight adversity by devising ways to overcome it in #Silence. #Enthusiasm

_____

_____

_____

95

Let the natural sounds of nature nurture you. #Silence #Enthusiasm

_____

_____

_____

96

Stop. Meditate. Let your feelings flow in dim light.
#Silence #Enthusiasm

_____

_____

_____

97

Let #Silence serve as a vehicle for the mind. #Enthusiasm

_____

_____

_____

98

Clear the beehive that is your mind. #Silence
#Enthusiasm

_____

_____

_____

99

Create your own rhythm. Breathe. It will slowly
manufacture #Enthusiasm. #Silence

_____

_____

_____

100

Breathe. Two rules. Inhale. Exhale. A simple
#EnthusiasmStarter. #Silence

_____

_____

_____

101

Breathe. Whatever your pace. Breathe. Let the air in your
lungs amass. #Silence #Enthusiasm

_____

_____

_____

102

Think, "Less go, more show." Allow the white space to
develop. #Silence #Enthusiasm

_____

_____

_____

103

Stop. Be quiet. Give yourself a chance at insight.
#Silence #Enthusiasm

_____

_____

_____

104

Let #Silence be a simple form of mental detox.
#Enthusiasm

_____

_____

_____

105

Look around. Measure your curiosity.
#Silence #Enthusiasm

_____

_____

_____

106

In #Silence brews heightened awareness. #Enthusiasm

_____

_____

_____

107

Zero has a way of adding up to much more.
#Silence #Enthusiasm

_____

_____

_____

108

Adjust. If you can't see it, hear it. If you can't hear it, taste it. If you can't taste it, smell it. If you can't smell it, FEEL IT. #Silence #Enthusiasm

---

109

Stop. Listen to the white space. You can't erase your past. So, welcome your future. #Silence #Enthusiasm

---

110

Account for your consciousness. What new sounds did you hear today? #Silence #Enthusiasm

_____

_____

_____

111

Practicing #Silence can be a rewarding and thus, worthwhile trend. #Enthusiasm

_____

_____

_____

112

Let the practice of #Silence represent a chance for the mind to rest. #Enthusiasm

_____

_____

_____

113

When you replace inappropriate monologue with #Silence, you've grown. #Enthusiasm

_____

_____

_____

114

Often, mending yourself begins with a plan developed in #Silence. #Enthusiasm

----

115

Practicing #Silence has a way of strengthening the power to react when making split-second decisions are crucial and to respond when impulsivity can be catastrophic. #Enthusiasm

----

Spending time with those we
#Trust represents a type of
continuing education.
#Enthusiasm

Fox Beyer

https://aha.pub/FACTS

Share the AHA messages from this book socially by going to
https://aha.pub/FACTS.

Section V

S-Find **Someone You Trust**

Is an enthusiastic mindset itself enough to surmount adversity? NO! So, what do we need to do? Surround ourselves with people we trust, those who listen, encourage, and challenge us, thereby strengthening our ability to navigate challenges WITH ENTHUSIASM!

F — Understand that when you FAIL, it doesn't make you a failure.

A — Embrace your AUTHENTICITY. Let people see your quirks and insecurities.

C — Learn from others, rather than COMPARING yourself to them.

T — "TURN off the noise" to allow the "white space"

S — Find SOMEONE you trust, who listens/builds you up/breaks you down when needed.

116

Those we #Trust pull us off the edge of catastrophe.
#Enthusiasm

_____

_____

_____

117

Those we #Trust tell us things about ourselves that
we don't want to hear, in an effort to make us better.
#Enthusiasm

_____

_____

_____

118

Those we #Trust know when it is time to listen.
#Enthusiasm

_____

_____

_____

119

Those we #Trust push us to set a high bar —
and raise it — every day. #Enthusiasm

_____

_____

_____

120

Credibility, responsibility, and accountability. Key elements of #Trust, #Growth, and #Enthusiasm.

_____

_____

_____

121

Those we #Trust stress the importance of initiative. #Enthusiasm

_____

_____

_____

122

Those we #Trust instill pride. #Enthusiasm

_____

_____

_____

123

#Trust: Knowing when to push, pull, or let be. #Enthusiasm

_____

_____

_____

124

Value relationships. They lead to results. #Trust #Enthusiasm

_____

_____

_____

125

A healthy balance between consequences and reinforcement is key to a relationship based on #Trust. #Enthusiasm

_____

_____

_____

126

Find someone who listens to your situation, kills the weeds, and waters the grass. #Trust #Enthusiasm

_____

_____

_____

127

Those we #Trust help us kill bad habits, erase self-doubt, and develop amateur schemes. #Enthusiasm

_____

_____

_____

128

Those we #Trust help us examine, collect, diagnose, and determine. #Enthusiasm

_____

_____

_____

129

Those we #Trust push, pull, and listen in the name of building mental toughness. #Enthusiasm

_____

_____

_____

130

Those we #Trust bolster our #Enthusiasm, helping us win with our "B" game.

_____

_____

_____

131

Those we #Trust help us adjust. #Enthusiasm

_____

_____

_____

132

Those we #Trust help us mend and reconstruct.
#Enthusiasm

_____

_____

_____

133

Those we #Trust help us develop in the wreckage of past
defeats. #Enthusiasm

_____

_____

_____

134

Those we #Trust stress perseverance. Try. Fail. Learn.
Grow. #Enthusiasm

_____

_____

_____

135

Those we #Trust know how to smother our fears.
#Enthusiasm

_____

_____

_____

136

Those we #Trust use words intended to guide us
to victory. #Enthusiasm

_____

_____

_____

137

Those we #Trust keep us from draining our #Enthusiasm.
With their help, we learn from the past rather than
harp on it.

_____

_____

_____

138

Those we #Trust help us differentiate between what is important and what is urgent. #Enthusiasm

_____

_____

_____

139

Spending time with those we #Trust represents a type of continuing education. #Enthusiasm

_____

_____

_____

140

When we invest time with those we #Trust,
we become more valuable to others. #Enthusiasm

_____

_____

_____

Epilogue

After completing my first week as a classroom teacher in 2005, the man who hired me called me into his office. I don't recall much about that meeting. What I do remember, however, will remain with me for a long time. After small talk and a short period of silence, he looked at me sternly. His words seemed to come out in slow motion:

"Your biggest tool is your enthusiasm."

He couldn't have been more right.

Almost fifteen years later, in September 2019, I sat behind a desk during second-period hall duty. My supervisor approached me with a wry smile on his face, as if he was about to deliver a message so daunting that he couldn't help but laugh. He glanced in both directions before sharing the news as straight-faced as he could:

"Fox, there are 988 class periods remaining in the school year."

I had to chuckle for a moment.

Then I thought, "How am I going to maintain enthusiasm through 988 more classes?" This led to a period of reflection. I thought deeply about my life and teaching career, essentially asking the question, "What are the things that I adhere to or refrain from that allow me to walk through the classroom door, instruct, assess, and inspire to the very best of my ability?"

Over the next few months, I came up with an acronym that most closely describes my approach, which became the title of this book.

- F — Understand that when you FAIL, it doesn't make you a failure.
- A — Embrace your AUTHENTICITY. Let people see your quirks and insecurities.
- C — Learn from others, rather than COMPARING yourself to them.
- T — "TURN off the noise" to allow the "white space"
- S —Find SOMEONE you trust, who listens/builds you up/breaks you down when needed.

Enjoy the journey, apply F.A.C.T.S., and attack adversity with vigor!

My best,
Fox

About the Author

Fox Beyer is a classroom teacher at Whippany Park High School (NJ). Since 2005, Fox has committed to his students through dedicating himself to servant leadership. He published *Letter Kindling: Igniting, Inspiring, and Evoking the Fire Within* in 2015. Now he's in his fourteenth season as a coach for the Atlantic League's Somerset Patriots, and he enjoys conveying the challenges of cerebral palsy through writing, speaking, and his *What's Your Inspiration* podcast.

AHA**that**®

THiNKaha has created AHAthat for you to share content from this book.

➲ Share each AHA message socially:
   https://aha.pub/FACTS

➲ Share additional content: **https://AHAthat.com**

➲ Info on authoring: **https://AHAthat.com/Author**

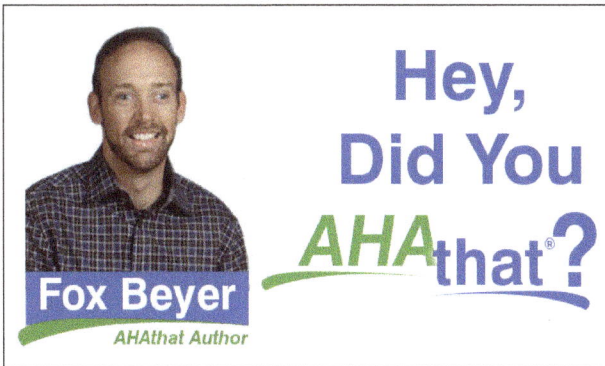

www.ingramcontent.com/pod-product-compliance
Lightning Source LLC
Chambersburg PA
CBHW042118190326
41519CB00030B/7541